T0194246

WHISPERS OF GOD'S LOVE

HOPE, FAITH, LOVE

Pamella P. Morrison

WESTBOW
PRESS®
A DIVISION OF THOMAS NELSON
& ZONDERVAN

Copyright © 2018 Pamella P. Morrison.

All rights reserved. No part of this book may be used or reproduced by
any means, graphic, electronic, or mechanical, including photocopying,
recording, taping or by any information storage retrieval system
without the written permission of the author except in the case of
brief quotations embodied in critical articles and reviews.

WestBow Press books may be ordered through booksellers or by contacting:

WestBow Press
A Division of Thomas Nelson & Zondervan
1663 Liberty Drive
Bloomington, IN 47403
www.westbowpress.com
1 (866) 928-1240

Because of the dynamic nature of the Internet, any web addresses or
links contained in this book may have changed since publication and
may no longer be valid. The views expressed in this work are solely those
of the author and do not necessarily reflect the views of the publisher,
and the publisher hereby disclaims any responsibility for them.

Any people depicted in stock imagery provided by Getty Images are
models, and such images are being used for illustrative purposes only.
Certain stock imagery © Getty Images.

Scripture taken from the King James Version of the Bible.

THE HOLY BIBLE, NEW INTERNATIONAL VERSION®,
NIV® Copyright © 1973, 1978, 1984, 2011 by Biblica, Inc.®
Used by permission. All rights reserved worldwide.

ISBN: 978-1-9736-3038-8 (sc)
ISBN: 978-1-9736-3039-5 (hc)
ISBN: 978-1-9736-3037-1 (e)

Library of Congress Control Number: 2018906798

Print information available on the last page.

WestBow Press rev. date: 08/02/2018

To my daughter, Jhanelle K. Brown.
Me for you, you for me, God for us.

CONTENTS

```
H           F              L
HOPE     FAITH     LOVE
P            I              V
E            T              E
             H
```

Author's Note

Life can be overwhelming as we go through our struggles and trials. Sometimes we become so despondent we feel weary, and our joy is diminished. I understand that it is not going to be like that always; every day affords me a new start.

"Morning by morning new mercies I see. What I needed the Lord has provided. Great is thy faithfulness unto me." ~Thomas Chisholm

Searching scriptures and devotions helps me to navigate and charter this channel of literature with a deeper understanding and declare the trust and dependence on Christ Jesus and learn how to lean on Him. The apostle Paul addressed the Corinthians, exhorting them in so much preaching and teaching. Paul mentioned in one instance, the trials and hardships he encountered on his various missionary journeys. His Christian faith guided and provided the spiritual and physical strength to overcome the inevitable. He saw that trusting God, who loved us enough to die for us, should give us reason of hope and faith to affirm and reflect on God's goodness, grace, and mercy. Despite our weaknesses, failures, and weariness, we must press on. It will take diligence through prayer with God's magnificent power and the guidance of the Holy Spirit to increase our faith.

Introduction

I pray this book will be an inspiration to all who read it. Maybe you have hopes and dreams and they were shattered. Perhaps you are lonely, feel lost, and believe no one cares. Jesus cares. He is a God of second chances and I believe miracles do happen. I called out to the Lord when I needed a closer fellowship with Him, and to this day I can call on Him night or day.

One Sunday morning in 2006, while I was listening to gospel music and attending to chores, I had my moment. I was awestruck when words rushed into my mind like a cascading waterfall. They were not from a song or book it was the Lord speaking words of encouragement to me. I immediately got a sheet of paper and started writing. This went on every Sunday morning for several weeks. Some weeks later, I compiled these verses in a notebook. In 2015 I started typing the verses with the intention of publishing the material, so it could be a blessing to others.

I recall when my daughter was less than a year old I would sit her on my knees, hold her hands to clap and sing the popular children's song "Jesus Loves Me." I have relied on the words of that song throughout life's journey. Let's praise God, worship Him, and listen to what He is whispering now. May God bless you, and may you find some words of encouragement to preserve your spirit in all circumstances.

When I See the Mountain

I am only a vessel made of clay.
My thoughts I dread from day to day.
I asked, Who am I, and where am I going?
But nothing seemed to come to my mind.
I looked in the distance.
I said to myself, I don't have a chance
If I intend to climb.
I want to climb over to the other side,
Whatever betide.
But my spirit stirred within.
My children, are you ready to begin?

My mind was made up; Father, hold my hand.
You promised to take me to the Promised Land.
Here I am, Lord. I see the mountain.
The distance, the height are all I can see.
Dear Lord, it was on the mountain

You paid the price for me
That I am redeemed.

At times my strength is weak,
And I want to flee.
But where would I go?
I know it was godly and unconditional love
Why You were sent from above
To us below.
To You, Lord, I look to teach me to follow.

Dear Lord, I stretch my hands to You.
There's no other help I know.
What I know is that I must spend
More time with You.
I know Your promises are there and true.
I know You will carry me through.

For ye shall go out with joy, and be led forth with peace; the mountains and the hills shall break forth before you into singing and all the trees of the field shall clap their hands.

~Isaiah 55:12

Waiting to Bloom

The grass grows,
The river flows,
The sun shines,
The rain falls,
The bird sings.

Lord, You are everywhere.
Why should we fear?
The tears drop.
The heart longs for Your love.
As the deer pants for streams of water so my soul pants
for you, my God ~Psalm 42:1
I cast my care on You.
I know You are faithful and true.
Dear Lord, You make things happen.
Lord, You are wonderful and many things more.
But Lord, why am I on the floor?

I have been waiting.

I have been waiting.

I have been waiting.

Lord, I want to be lifted up from this despair
To see a sky that is clear.
The flowers bloom as in spring.
As the flowers bloom and receive the sunshine of your glory
Dear Lord, shine on me.

Flowers of My Soul

Spring.
Summer.
Autumn.
Winter.

Lord, You are perfect.
You made everything and everyone
For a purpose.
The flowers bloom,
But we are so overshadowed by gloom.
It may be hard to understand,
But for all of us,
You have a plan.

Dear Lord, I see Your beauty in nature's showers,
The rose, and the magnolia flowers.
Thank You for the beauty as the petals unfolds.
Thank You for the treasures untold.
Thank You for Your grace to fill my soul.

With You, Lord, my soul has been refreshed.
You make things happen, and I am blessed.

Lord, when I'm overwhelmed, and my spirit droops and wilts like a flower,
Your divine spirit gives me hope.
I am able to cope.
Lord, You never fail.
I know I can prevail.

Consider how the wild flowers grow. They do not labor or spin. Yet I tell you, not even Solomon in all his splendor was not dressed like one of these. ~ Luke 12: 27

Someday

What day is it?

Why do we clamor for it?

Will it come?

How will we know it is here?

Will it be bright and fair?

Will it be one we want to share?

Aren't those big questions?

Sure.

But we always want to know more.

Not so long ago,

Seems like only yesterday,

A little girl saw me in my struggles to make ends meet.

But we never accept defeat.

We sing, we laugh, and we always feel that someday things will be better.

When and how, we do not know,

But we trust in the One to whom everything belongs.

So what can go wrong?

A child not so long ago
Said to her mother,
"Oh, Mother, I love you.
Oh, Mother, peek-a-boo I see you.
A sigh escapes with a smile on her face. Someday things
are going to get easier, I do believe we'll arrive someday
When God makes a way.
These anxieties and cares will fade away.
So we know someday
will be near.
Just trust and obey,
Have faith,
Have hope,
Hold to hope like a rope
Because the One whom is strong is holding on.
Then someday will turn into today.

*I*nspiration

When you see the word "inspiration"
What comes to your mind?
To me, the awesome power of God and the Holy Spirit.
O Lord, You are holy.
O Lord, You are majestic.
To God all honor and glory be given.

Lives have been changed in the past and
Lives are changing today
Because we draw comfort from You.
Those lives You have touched are filled vessels.
With words, the weak of heart imparts.
Love is a gift for the past, present, and future.
David the psalmist, a great inspirator
A man said to be after God's own heart.
Looked at himself, saw himself, and found himself.
We too can self-reflect and be a beacon of inspiration.
God's Word reveals to us great and precious promises.

God's Word empowers us and lead us to a path of faith.

Thy words, O Lord, give light and life.

As I seek Thee, O Lord,

Help me not to lean on my own understanding

But let You direct my path.

Inspiration #2

I — Invest in reaching out to others.

N — New mercies every morning I see.

S — Seek the Lord while He is near.
   Seek Him with your whole heart.

P — Pray to the heavenly Father
   because prayer changes things.

I — In all things give thanks to the Lord of Hosts.

R — Raise the banner of hope.
   Reach out and touch the Lord as He passes by;
   He is not too busy to hear your heart's cry.

A — Abide under the shadow of the Almighty.
   Anoint my head with Your holy oil, O Lord.

T — Trust in the Lord with all your heart.

I — Inadequacy will drive you to be fainthearted, but
   God's divine opportunities are adequate and will
   enable us to realize our greatest potentials.

O — Over the mountain we want to go, but make
   yourself available to be a vessel to be used in the

Master's plan. He will inspire and motivate you by His power and faithfulness, and your life will not be the same.

N — Never give up, my child, when the struggles are overwhelming; Jesus will carry you.

The darkest part of night is just before dawn.

Jesus will be your lighthouse.

He will be your guide.

I will guide you in the way of wisdom and lead you along straight paths. When you walk, your steps will not be hampered; when you run, you will not stumble. Hold on to instruction, do not let go; guard it well, for it is your life. ~Proverbs 4: 11-13

In Time

Have you been waiting?
I have.
Have you been praying?
I have.
Have you been weak?
I have.
Have you been hesitant to speak?
I have.
Have you been weary?
I have.
Have you been tired?
I have.
Have you been in line to be hired?
I have.

What next?

So much more not in the text

That can be easily taken out of context.

So let not pretend,

It is so easy to defend.

But the Lord is defender of all.

Let us be of good courage.

Wait on Him.

It is no secret what He can do.

He can right all wrongs—in time.

Because His time is perfect.

Learn to discover to walk by faith.

Let Him be in control.

He can make us whole.

Trust in Him at all times, O people; pour out your hearts to Him, for God is our refuge. ~Psalm 62:8

Attitude

There is a word.
Do you know it?
Can you say it?
Can you spell it?
Here it is.
It comes from within.
It is
"Attitude."
It might seem a simple word,
But it has a big meaning.
So let us get it!
But have the right one.
Are you ready?
It's up to you to make it work.
Here and now, let us nurture good attitude.

A — Always look to the author and finisher of our faith.

T — Through Christ, the impossible can become possible.

T — Trust in the Lord; Bible texts can be your compass, and your guide.

I — Improve your thinking.

T — Turn your thoughts to the things that are honest, pure, and true.

U — Use me, Lord. You can use me as that vessel to do what You want me to do.

D — Destiny will eventually come through

Because God is standing by. He already has the master plan.

E — Exercise compassion, patience, faith and trust.

Each of you should look not only to your own interests, but also to the interests of others. Your attitude should be the same as that of Christ Jesus. ~ Philippians 2: 4-5

Moments

Have you ever thought of a moment in time?
One you want to cherish or forget?
Be it glad.
Be it sad.
Our Father in heaven wants us to experience things in
life
To make us mature.
He does not withhold any good thing from us, for sure.
That moment He turns water into wine
Because He is heavenly, and He is divine.
When our lives get dreary,
and we are weary.
Just call on the One who sustains.
Just claim victory in Jesus' name.

Many times, we have storms.
The tides rage and the waves roll.
But we have an anchor.

The Lord keeps us safe and we are under His control.

When you have your moments and your hopes dashes.

Make your call to glory.

Jesus is on the line;

You need not worry.

The line will not be busy.

He will answer every time.

Trust and obey.

Do not doubt.

He is the one and only who knows us inside out.

He leads us right, not wrong.

Help us Lord, to know to whom we belong.

Now dear Lord, we humbly request,

Please put in our hearts a joyful song.

Hope

Hope is …
He is …
Here,
There,
Everywhere.
It does not take the rules of scientists.
It is from the one in whom the Word was manifest.
It is not a test.
It is not chess;
There is no pawn to move.
But it is the assurance from above,
Given by God, who is love.
Our loving Lord, who is the greatest,
Is able and ready to bless.

I shed my tears.
I cast out all fears.
His praise I sing.

To Jesus I cling.

I am learning to lean

On the One who has come to redeem.

Cradle me in Your arms, O Lord, and comfort me.

You are my hope.

Because of You, I am able to cope.

With You in the vessel, I can smile at the storms.

When I seem to be sinking in the deep,

When it is hard to sleep,

I am grateful for the reminder

That sorrow or heartache may be hard to endure,

But joy comes in the morning.

Hope will transform to new joy, contentment, and peace.

Hope is eternal.

Eternal hope is in God.

Hope in God today, can reveal tomorrow's blessings.

The Prodigal

Who are you?
What are you?
Where are you?

I am the one who is down and out.
I am on the mountain of doubt.
I am in the pig sty,
Just merely getting by.
Listen, listen, listen.
Have you not heard?
Have you not seen?

Come, my child,
You have long wasted time.
You can now be reinstated in the fold.
Yes, He's the shepherd who seeks and saves the lost.
Yes, at any cost.
Here, "Take my hand and arise,

He paid the price at Calvary.

Salvation is full and free."

He is waiting at the door.

Yes, there is room for more.

For you know the grace of our Lord Jesus Christ, that though he was rich, yet for your sakes he became poor, so that you through his poverty might become rich. ~ 2 Corinthians 8: 9

A Child

I'm a child of God.

The tempest is wild.

O Lord, let me in Your love abide.

I need You more than ever by my side,

I will stop,

I will look,

I will listen.

Lord, can You see me on the track?

I don't want to look back.

I want to make heaven my home.

Hear my cry; hear my call.

Please do not leave me alone.

To You I tell my story.

To You belongs the glory.

Help me to put away my worry.

My Father,

To You I humbly bow.

Your grace I need this hour.

Father, please help me now.

How great is the love the Father has lavished on us, that we should be called children of God! And that is what we are! ~1 John 3: 1

Journey

I can see.

Jesus said, "follow Me, and I will make you fishers of men." ~Mark 1: 17

He came from Nazareth to Galilee,

He caused the lame to walk,

The dumb to talk,

The blind to see.

The road was rocky and steep.

The path sometimes very muddy and deep.

In the shadows of the palm,

The followers could not be calm.

He rode on

In majesty,

Knowing He is the Son,

And His Father's will must be done.

In the garden, hearts were sad,

But this journey was destined planned.

He paid the price for you and me.
Praise the Lord, salvation full and free.

He embraced this prophesied event.
At Gethsemane He prayed.
On the cross He gave up the Ghost.
On the third day He arose.
All was not lost because there's the Holy Spirit.

He lives, He lives, He lives.
The one who came,
Not for wealth or fame,
But to seek and save the lost.
He is Jesus Christ,
The loving Savior
Who blesses and forgives.
He reigns supreme.
He is divine.
He is alive, He is alive, He is alive.
Hallelujah to the King.

See Me

I am in the mirror.
I am the one in sorrow,
And I want to know,
Where shall I go?
What shall I do?
I need the strength and abiding faith.
Yes, Lord, You came that we will have life eternal.

Lord, You love us more than our paternal.
You are the Rock of ages.
You are wiser than sages.
You are the calm in the storm.
You are the one who transforms.
You are the Holy One.

I see me.

You see me.

I am on my knee.

Your love is full and free.

See me.

I am behind the mirror,

Not looking, not knowing

Who or what I am.

Wondering what I see.

At the face I want to look;

All my courage it took.

What do others see?

Not sure of what I see, what they see,

Or what they want me to be.

Getting old and not bold,

I've opened pages for messages to be told.

Experience struggles, being tattered and torn.

In the midst, His blessings will unfold.

Sometimes so confused from within,

Don't know why or where to begin.

I seem to be walking a lonely pathway,

From morning to night, and night turns to day.

I do pray,
Lord, help me not stray.
I have friends who are far away.
You are near and everywhere.
Then why do I despair?
Lord, help me to see me.
Do I know but am afraid to show?
I am just a broken vessel,
Waiting and wanting You to repair me.

I am asking You, Lord,
To come by here.
I need You to be near.
I want You to find me.
I want You to see me.
I know what You can do for me.
I know it was Good Friday
When, on the cross, You gave Your all.
The day does not matter.
You did the will of Your Father.
Dear Lord, when on others You are calling,
Do not pass me by.
Hear my humble cry.

You see me,
You find me,
You know me; hear my plea.
I am just waiting for the Jubilee.

Hold On!

Hope,
Hope,
Hope.

God who is a constant source of hope.

In Him is my faith to hold on, to cope.

I know that Man from Galilee

Whose gift is love.

He has an outstretched hand.

He places us in the hollow of His palm.

He rescues us from all alarm.

Look at David and Goliath;

See: Shadrach, Meshach, and Abednego.

These were men of old.

Their story was told.

They were courageous.

What they did was not spontaneous,

But they trusted in God and did right.
With their faith and trust in God, they won the fight.

You may be dejected
Because you have been rejected.
Believe in the Lord Jesus Christ;
You will not be a loser.
You are a winner.
The Giver is in your corner.

If you are on the rough side of the mountain,
Just ask for the strength to go on;
Your strength He will renew.
You must hold on.
Remember Jesus made it all the way.
He did not come to stay;
He came to give the victory.
Hold on.
Some may go through the water,
Some may go through the fire,
But all go through the blood.
Jesus paid it all; a sacrifice to rescue you and me.
He is not going to let you go.
His arm is strong;

His army is mighty.

He knows where you belong.

The mountain can't be too high.

Hold His hand;

He will help you to hold on.

There is hope for everyone.

That Man is Jesus.

He gave His life for us

So that we can have life eternal.

Hail Him, praise Him and shout for Him,

Jesus, Jesus, Jesus.

He is the answer.

Hope comes from the risen Christ.

I have hope.

You have hope.

I have a future.

You have a future.

We all have a future in the Lord if we hold on.

Thank You Jesus.

Why are you downcast, O my soul? Why so disturbed within me? Put your hope in God, for I will yet praise Him, my Savior and my God. ~Psalm 42:5

A Life for Living

Live for Jesus.
This matters and will last,
Use the entrance, this too can pass.
Listen to the knock at the door of your heart.
Be wise and answer.
A knock from the Savior to the room of your heart.
Open the door.
To make you secure.

Life's experience levels and phases.
With many pleasant and unpleasant cases.
He will enter through that door.
In your heart He will pour
Love that will light up your life.
The unconditional love
Comes from above.

He loves you first, is where it began,

Free from a burden of sin.

Just ask Him to forgive.

He gave his life to make you live

Ask Him to come in, and His rich promises will be fulfilled

Reflect on the power that rolled away the stone.

A mighty triumph, He arose.

Celebrate because no stone is too huge or heavy.

My Lord can roll away any burden you bear.

Let Him enter through that door of your heart.

Whether you are rich or poor,

Christ is the one to adore.

Come!

Have a new beginning.

*Therefore, if anyone is in Christ, he is a new creation;
the old is gone, the new has come! ~2 Corinthians 5: 17*

Lifted

Get up!

Your morning has come.

When you get down on your knees,

When you are lifted up,

You will be lifted up by the Holy One.

The Holy Spirit

Your brokenness will see

In the gutter.

Not a word you can utter

In the mire.

Get on spiritual fire.

Even if you are afflicted,

Let your spirit be led.

Get up! Rise up!

Your morning has come.

The Lord will not abandon you whether you're young or old.

What do you have to fear?

What do you have to dread?

Lean on the everlasting arms of Jesus.

He cares!

Jesus said to the man, "Take up your bed and walk."

It did not take might

To overcome the fight,

Only an assurance of faith.

Faith can work for you and me.

That man by the gate did not hesitate.

He did not debate.

He stood up and leaped for joy.

And he gave his praises; he could not be silent.

His joy was complete.

Just believe in Jesus Christ.

He can make things right.

I will lift up my eyes to the hills-where does my help come from? My help comes from the Lord the maker of heaven and earth. ~Psalm 121: 1-2

Don't Give Up

You have a friend in Jesus.
Have a little talk with Him.
Do you feel like you are going around a bend?
Or have reached a dead end?
Believe in miracles.
Remember you can call on Jesus,
He will lift you up when you fall.
He will come through for you.
Rest assure He will do more.
It's no secret what God can do.

You can only see your situation,
Your heart palpitates,
You wallow in pity, and desire to hate.
Everything seems so hopeless and so discouraged,
What is my fate?
Where is the solution?
Jesus, You are my only plea.

You can set me free.

It was done at Calvary.

Now, dear Lord, please draw me closer to Thee.

May Your grace reach this fainting heart.

Don't leave me to wander all alone.

Let me come to Your sacred throne.

I do believe, I now believe,

That You died for me.

Just a word from You, and I can be whole.

But I can do all things through Christ who strengthens me. ~Philippians 4:13

Mothers of Zion: The Beacon

Mother, Mother, Mother.
You are bright,
You are fair,
You believe in God,
You care,
You share,
The Lord's words you declare.
You tell of His love
And that He is the light of the world.

You pray without ceasing
For the young and the old,
For those in despair, and even grieving souls,
For those in the dark where the tempest is raging,
For people in a world of turmoil where wars are waging,
For others out in the cold, with stories untold.

You have a passion to lay all on the altar.

You pray to God for answers.

You know prayer empowers.

You know prayer prepares you for the battle,

But the battle is not yours; it's the Lord's.

And no weapon formed against you shall prosper.

Know that prayer is a key to opening doors.

You know that the prayer is a light to break through the darkness.

Prayer changes things.

The conflict may be long,

Put on your armor and be strong.

Seek to gain the victory the Lord your God will fight for you.

Take the helmet of salvation and the sword of the Spirit, which is the word of God. And pray in the Spirit on all Occasions with all kinds of prayers and requests. With this in mind, be alert and always keep on praying for all saints. Pray also for me, that whenever I open my mouth, words may be given me so that I will fearlessly make known the mystery of the **gospel. ~Ephesians 6:17-19**

The Lighthouse

The ship has sailed.
It is in the deep.
The billows and tempest toss.
The pitch of night,
As given a fright,
The atmosphere is drear,
The thought of peril is near.

In the mist the lighthouse stands.
The situation may seem hopeless,
But the light is coming through the mist.
The surge is subsiding.
No matter what, His deep love is abiding.

The sea He can calm.

The darkness He can dispel.

Thank God for the lighthouse

To bring hope,

To bring peace,

To bring joy,

To bring the ship safely to the shore.

In His love I will safely abide evermore.

Your word is a lamp to my feet and a light for my path. ~Psalm 119: 105

The Lifeline

There is a lifeline; give a shout-out.
Don't give up; don't you bow out.
The world seems to be passing you by.
There is nothing that seems to make you satisfied.

In distress,
Wondering, *Where is success?*
Don't you cry, don't you fret,
The best is yet to come.
No matter how far you have drifted away,
Just reach out and pray.
Your lifeline is just a breath away.
Be patient,
Be penitent.
He is omnipresent,
He is heaven sent.

There is no height, width, or depth,

No boundaries;

He is from coast to coast.

The lifeline is here and everywhere.

His strong, loving arms will pull you through.

Go for it; hold on to His unchanging hand.

Your choice makes a difference.

He is here to your rescue.

Be lifted; come ashore.

He is willing to restore.

In my distress I called to the Lord; I cried to my God for help. From his temple he heard my voice; my cry came before him, into his ears. ~Psalm 18: 6

The Valley

To the left,
To the right,
The mountain casts its shadows.
There is a valley surrounded by the meadows.

You try to be calm,
But the alarm of the eruption.
Yes, it is the volcano;
Sight the inferno.
What shall I say?
What shall I do?
You listen.
You watch.
You are no match.
So be still.
The Master's will is to be amidst a fire.

In the fiery fury,
You may feel weary.
The Lord covers you still.
You'll be safe.
His promises He will fulfill.
For me, dear Lord, Thy will be done.
In me Your work has begun.
Show me the light of the sun.
The victory is mine when the race is run.
It is not for the swift but the one who endures.
Dear Lord, the battle is all Yours.
In me make Thy Holy Spirit pour.
That's how I know I can make it
With you by my side I can take it.

The Wilderness

"What is a wilderness?"
You might ask.
"Where is the wilderness?
How did I reach there?"
Don't you despair
For there is someone who cares.
He knows where you are,
Be it in the ravine or perhaps in the dark,
Your heavenly Father sees and knows.
He's not very far
He understands your struggles.
Do not feel defeated.
Stretch out your hand.
The struggles are almost over.
To be lifted from the gloom,
Feel the divine power.
It is now the accepted hour.
Dear Lord, where You lead me I will follow.

I give you my heart full of anguish and sorrow.

Precious love for one and all

Thank the Lord for answering my call.

Please Lord; lead me gently through the path to light.

Be my constant guiding light

Direct me as I find my way,

Singing encouraging songs throughout the day.

Jesus loves me, this I know, for the Bible tells me so!

~Anna Bartlett Warner & William Batchelder Bradbur

Going through to Get Out

Is it through Edom?
Is it through a valley?
Is it through the Red Sea?

There is never a walk so dreary.
All the cares of yesterday, today are here.
Sometimes trials seem so hard to bear
For body, mind, and soul.
Lord, give me that reviving touch to make me whole.
Prove the one who calls you to deliverance,
Who has helped you to overcome anxious moments,
fears, and tears.
He promises to guide you through your trials,
Over the mountains;
Yes, you may be going through the valleys.
He guides His children to blessings' overflow

As we seek refuge in Jesus here below.

He claims us has His own.

Because of whom You are, Lord,

I give You glory; I give You praise.

I am going to make it through, to get out.

By Your strength, O Lord, I can stand.

You are keeping me in the hollow of Your palm.

I know I must let my mind rest on You.

I thank You, Jesus.

No weapon formed against you shall prosper. ~ Isaiah 54:17

All the Father has for me shall be mine.

I am casting my cares on You, Lord.

I know You care a lot for me.

Your praise I shall always sing

For You are divine.

Strength for Today— Hope for Tomorrow

Dear Lord, I am here.

What a privilege to come to You.

I know You are near and not too busy to hear us call.

I thank God for the gospels and the solid rock on which I stand.

I am asking You to hold my hand.

Living words that flourish in my soul.

When trials arise, and struggles appear,

Help me, Lord, not to despair

But look to Thee, my ever-constant source.

Sometimes life seems to be like a winding road.

With lots of burden and heavy loads

Thank You for Your love and assurance,

Guidance on the course of life, and for watching over me,

Guiding every step I take.

Eternal and heavenly Father, the one who provides and blesses,

I express my gratitude for things great and small.

I rejoice for salvation and your everlasting mercy.

Lord, because of You, I am able to cope.

I believe forever in the blessed hope.

I know I will receive my blessings.

I hear Your words, O Master,

Instructing me to love my neighbors as myself,

In this I will abide and in the future I will apply his teachings and his word.

But I am not alone.

My Lord is not only standing by

He is my guide

My hope,

My stay.

To Him I always pray

So I know I will grow from strength to strength, day by day.

The Lord is my strength and my shield, my heart trusts in him, and I am helped. My heart leaps for joy and I will give thanks to him in song. The Lord is the strength of his people, a fortress of salvation for his anointed one. ~Psalm 28: 7-8

Miracle

When I look back over my life,
I see God rescued me.
I didn't know then,
All I could do is question why?
But in mind,
He is faithful,
And He is kind.
I know without a doubt
That He is mine.
It's His miracle for all
And for all who believe.
So don't sit and ponder, *Why?*
Just remember the one on the throne
Will not leave you alone.
He sees you as His own.
A prize to bestow.
He never fails.
Believe in His words.

He will guide you with His eye.

Just give Him a start.

With God on your side, He will never part.

Have great expectations and anticipation.

With faith of miracles within your heart.

You are the God who performs miracles; you display your power among the peoples. ~ Psalm 77:14

Scriptures

Hope

"For you have been my hope O Sovereign Lord, my confidence since my youth." ~Psalm 71:5

"We have this hope as an anchor for the soul, firm and secure."~ Hebrews 6:19

"For everything that was written in the past was written to teach us, so that through endurance and the encouragement of the Scriptures we might have hope." ~Romans 15:4

Faith

"Now faith is being sure of what we hope for and certain of what we do not see." ~Hebrews 11:1

"Let us fix our eyes on Jesus, the author and perfecter of our faith." ~Hebrews 12:2

"Let us hold unswervingly to the hope we profess, for he who promised is faithful." ~Hebrews 10:23

Love

"Dear friends, let us love one another, for love comes from God." ~ 1John 4:7

"For God so loved the world that he gave his one and only Son, that whoever believes in him shall not perish but have eternal life." ~John 3:16

"And now these three remain: faith, hope and love. But the greatest of these is love."

~ 1 Corinthians 13:13

"Give thanks to the Lord, for he is good His love endures forever." ~Psalm 136:1

Prayer

Dear Lord, I thank You for loving me. Thank You for leading me into peace of mind. Thank You for a blessed hope for my future and Your children. I thank You, dear Lord, for the battles You fought for me, the mountains to climb, the valleys and plains to pass through, and the rivers to wade through. O God, to You all the praise and honor and glory for Your love and blessings. Father, I trust in Your Word and timing to make things happen. O Heavenly Father, we know that Your promises are sure and has we cast our cares on You and put our trust in You, by faith we will overcome. Thank You, O Lord, for being with us in our trials and helping us to grow through difficult circumstances. In Jesus' name, Amen.

References

The Holy Bible
King James Version
New International Version

Printed in the United States
By Bookmasters